MY ELECTED REPRESENTATIVES WENT TO WASHINGTON

Tom Toles is distributed internationally by Universal Press Syndicate.

My Elected Representatives Went to Washington copyright © 1993 by Buffalo News. All rights reserved. Printed in the United States of America. No part of this book may be used or reproduced in any manner whatsoever without written permission except in the case of reprints in the context of reviews. For information write Andrews and McMeel, a Universal Press Syndicate Company, 4900 Main Street, Kansas City, Missouri 64112.

ISBN: 0-8362-1716-0

Library of Congress Catalog Card Number: 92-75354

T002095

MY ELECTED REPRESENTATIVES WENT TO WASHINGTON

cartoons by Tom TOLES

Andrews and McMeel
A Universal Press Syndicate Company
Kansas City

To Rose and Bud

May 20, 1991

June 4, 1991

June 9, 1991

June 12, 1991

June 17, 1991

Have-a-heart Sununu trap

June 27, 1991

The fuel-efficiency/safety issue

Videotape footage of a collision between a semi and a full-sized car, demonstrating that full-sized cars are unsafe, and that everyone should drive a tractor trailer, despite the somewhat *lower* fuel efficiency.

UNLESS, OF COURSE, YOU CAN AFFORD A LOCOMOTIVE.—

July 7, 1991

12

July 8, 1991

Situation Room at Rand McNally -- 1992 Edition

July 30, 1991

August 5, 1991

August 6, 1991

August 11, 1991

The reason Verbal SAT scores are at an all-time low.

September 1, 1991

Economic Bungee Jumping

September 2, 1991

September 8, 1991

September 11, 1991

September 12, 1991

September 23, 1991

September 24, 1991

September 26, 1991

October 1, 1991

October 29, 1991

Five living U.S. presidents do a reading
at the Reagan library

November 6, 1991

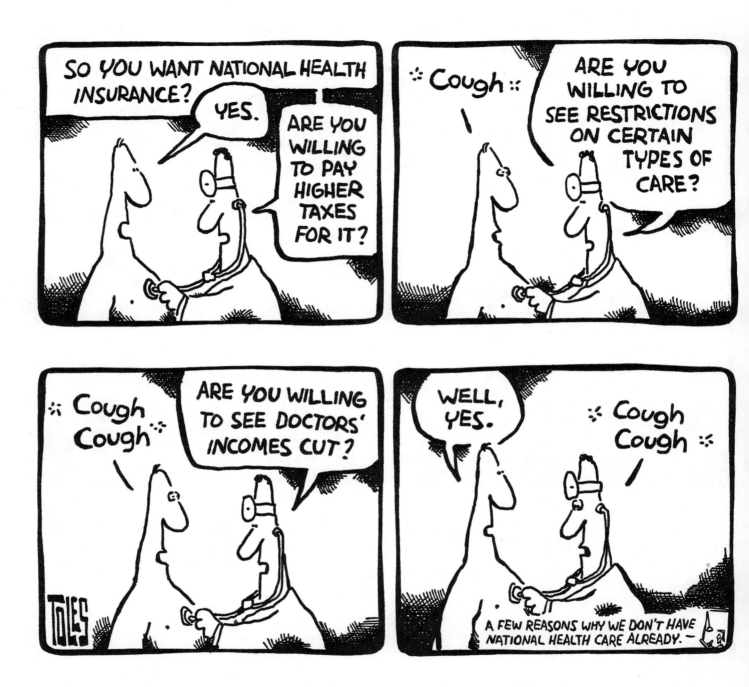

November 11, 1991

November 12, 1991

November 18, 1991

November 19, 1991

Superpower competition: the final chapter.

November 21, 1991

November 25, 1991

December 1, 1991

December 2, 1991

Before

IRELAND · BRITAIN · NOR. · SWED. · DENMARK · NETHERLANDS · GERMANY · BELGIUM · LUXEMBOURG · SWITZERLAND · LIECHTENSTEIN · FRANCE · MONACO · AUSTRIA · PORTUGAL · SPAIN · ANDORRA · ITALY

U.S.S.R.

After

EUROPE · ESTONIA · LATVIA · LITHUANIA · BYELORUSSIA · RUSSIA · SIBERIA · YAKUT · MOLDAVIA · UKRAINE · KAZAKHSTAN · UZBEKISTAN · KIRGHIZ · GEORGIA · ARMENIA · AZERBAIJAN · TURKMENISTAN · TAJIK

TOLES

BEFORE AND AFTER WHAT? —

BEFORE AND AFTER YOU BLINKED. —

December 4, 1991

December 5, 1991

The Emperor's New Office

December 10, 1991

December 12, 1991

January 2, 1992

January 5, 1992

January 13, 1992

January 21, 1992

February 2, 1992

February 3, 1992

February 9, 1992

February 24, 1992

February 27, 1992

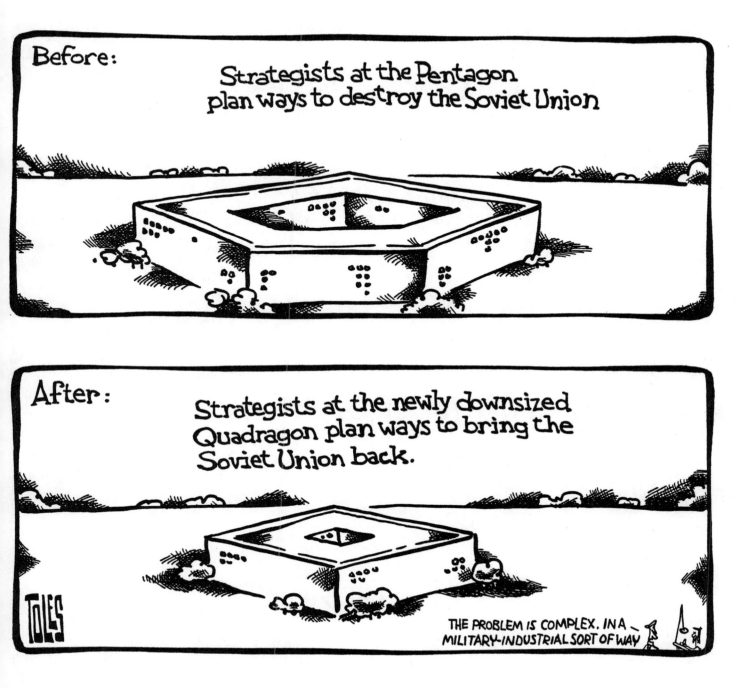

Before: Strategists at the Pentagon plan ways to destroy the Soviet Union

After: Strategists at the newly downsized Quadragon plan ways to bring the Soviet Union back.

THE PROBLEM IS COMPLEX. IN A MILITARY-INDUSTRIAL SORT OF WAY

TOLES

March 11, 1992

55

Grand Old Party Pooper

March 15, 1992

March 17, 1992

March 22, 1992

March 23, 1992

Cuomo rehearsing his answer to whether he wants to be vice-president.

March 29, 1992

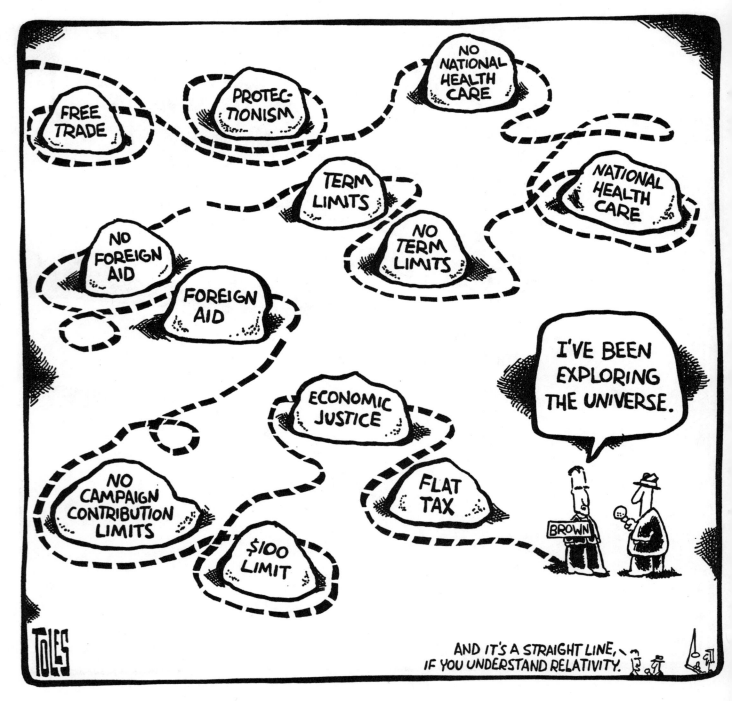

April 3, 1992

April 5, 1992

April 8, 1992

April 13, 1992

April 20, 1992

May 6, 1992

May 13, 1992

May 15, 1992

May 17, 1992

May 27, 1992

May 28, 1992

Unclestiltskin

If the Indians had had an immigration policy.

DOES THIS MEAN WE'RE NOT INVITED FOR THANKSGIVING?

June 1, 1992

June 5, 1992

June 8, 1992

June 10, 1992

THE WORLD'S ONLY —
REMAINING BLOOPERPOWER.

June 14, 1992

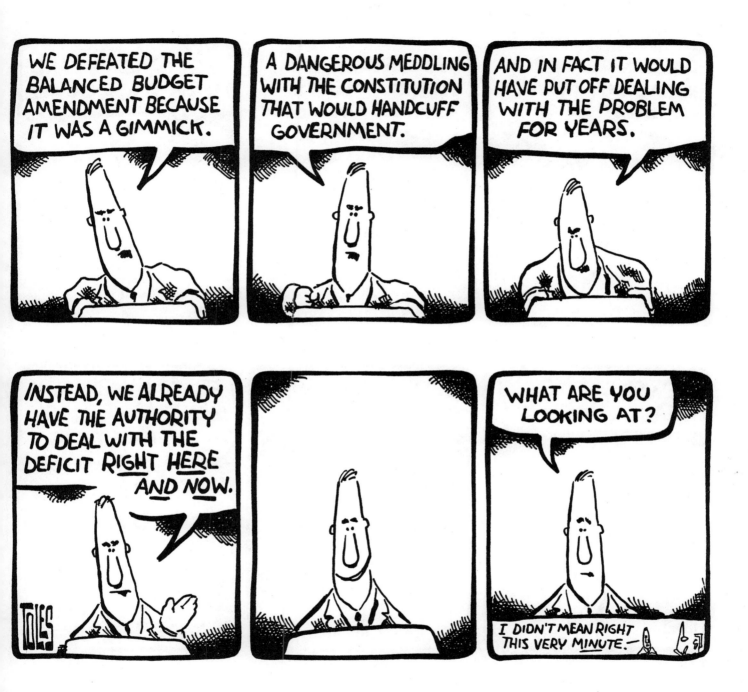

June 22, 1992

June 23, 1992

July 8, 1992

Preparing for the V.P. debate

July 13, 1992

July 18, 1992

July 28, 1992

July 31, 1992

August 3, 1992

August 6, 1992

Ethnic "cleansing"

IT'S A DIRTY JOB, BUT—
NOBODY HAS TO DO IT

August 9, 1992

August 20, 1992

August 23, 1992

Suddenly, the President becomes interested in job training for the unemployed.

August 31, 1992

Bobby Fischer is back

September 2, 1992

September 8, 1992

95

September 9, 1992

September 10, 1992

September 11, 1992

September 13, 1992

September 18, 1992

September 22, 1992

September 25, 1992

September 28, 1992

September 30, 1992

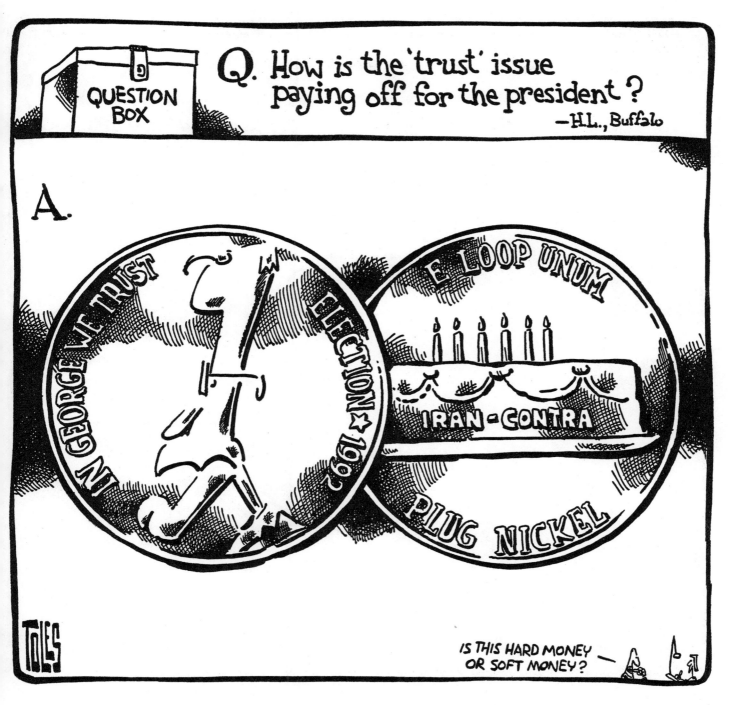

October 2, 1992

October 4, 1992

October 6, 1992

October 14, 1992

October 16, 1992

October 18, 1992

THE MAGIC OF
THE MARKETPLACE

October 23, 1992

111

October 25, 1992

Keeping Busy

October 27, 1992

Conspiracy Theory #2,437

October 28, 1992

115

The Vision Thing

November 1, 1992

ANOTHER SUCCESSFUL MISSION, PUTTING UP A TINY SATELLITE THAT COULD HAVE BEEN DONE FAR CHEAPER WITH A SMALL UNMANNED ROCKET.

Shuttle

AND WE OBJECT TO SUGGESTIONS THAT IT WAS JUST ANOTHER NEEDLESS, EXPENSIVE EXCUSE TO PUT PEOPLE IN SPACE.

$$$$

WE ALSO DID IMPORTANT WORK TO PREPARE FOR THE MANNED U.S. SPACE STATION.

November 2, 1992

SPACE PORKY
THE MISSIONLESS MANNED SPACE STATION

EVEN BIGGER, NEEDLESS EXPENSIVE EXCUSE TO PUT PEOPLE IN SPACE.

AMERICA'S SACRED PIG.

November 6, 1992

November 9, 1992

November 10, 1992

November 12, 1992

November 15, 1992

November 18, 1992

November 20, 1992

November 22, 1992

November 24, 1992

November 27, 1992